KIDS
CALLIGRAPHY
ADVENTURES
AF364732

Introduction to Calligraphy

Hello, young artist!

Welcome to the exciting world of calligraphy! You might be wondering, "What exactly is calligraphy?" Well, calligraphy is the art of creating beautiful and stylish letters and words. It's like drawing, but with letters!

Why is Calligraphy Fun and Useful?

Be Creative: Calligraphy lets you play with letters just like you play with colors and shapes. You can turn simple words into amazing artworks. Imagine writing your name in a super cool way that no one else does!

Make Special Gifts: You can use calligraphy to make special cards for your friends and family. Imagine how happy they will be to get a beautiful birthday card made by you!

Learn Something New: Just like learning to ride a bike or to swim, learning calligraphy is a new skill. It's fun to learn how to hold the pen and make different kinds of strokes.

It's Like a Game: Practicing calligraphy is like playing a game where you try to make the neatest and most beautiful letters. And the best part? There are no winners or losers – everyone has fun and creates something beautiful!

A Great Hobby: Calligraphy can become a hobby that you enjoy doing in your free time. It's relaxing and lets you express your feelings and creativity.

So, grab your pen, and let's start this fun journey into the world of calligraphy. Are you ready to make some magic with letters? Let's go!

What You Will Need

Hey there, little calligrapher! Before we start our adventure in the world of beautiful letters, let's talk about the tools you'll need. Don't worry, they are all super fun and easy to use!

Calligraphy Markers or Pens: These are not just any pens – they are like magic wands for writing! Calligraphy markers have a special tip that helps you make thick and thin lines. You can choose colorful markers to make your writing even more fun!

Thick Paper: Regular paper is fine, but thicker paper is awesome for calligraphy. It's like a smooth playground for your markers, where they can slide and dance without any bumps!

Ruler and Pencil: Sometimes, we need a little help to make straight lines. A ruler and a pencil are great friends for that. You can draw light lines on your paper to help guide your writing.

Eraser: Just like in drawing, sometimes we need to erase our pencil lines or little oopsies. So, an eraser is a handy friend to have.

Practice Sheets (Optional): These are special sheets with dotted lines that can help you practice. Think of them like training wheels when you're learning to ride a bike. They're great for beginners!

Colorful Stickers and Glitter (Just for Fun!): After you're done writing, you might want to decorate your work with some stickers or a little bit of glitter. It's all about making your art as unique as you are!

Now that you have all your cool tools, you're ready to become a young calligraphy wizard! Let's open the door to a world where letters are not just letters, but a way to make your imagination come to life! Are you excited? I sure am! Let's get started!

First Shapes and Strokes

Now that we have our tools, it's time to start the real fun – making your first shapes and strokes! These are the building blocks of calligraphy, kind of like the ABCs of drawing cool letters. Let's dive in!

Straight Lines:

Let's start simple. Take your calligraphy pen and draw some straight lines on your paper. Try to make them as straight as an arrow! You can draw them horizontal, like the horizon, or vertical, like a tall tree.

Ready, set, draw!

Curvy Lines:

After practicing straight lines, let's make some waves! Draw some curvy lines, like gentle waves in the ocean. These curves will help you when you start making letters.

Ready, set, draw!

Circles and Ovals:

Circles and ovals are like the round shapes of letters. Try drawing some. They don't have to be perfect – just round and happy!

Ready, set, draw!

Ups and Downs:

Now let's try making some lines that go up and then down, kind of like little hills. This will teach you how to move your pen up and down smoothly.

Ready, set, draw!

Connecting the Dots:

Imagine there are tiny dots on your paper. Try connecting them with your lines – straight, curvy, or wavy. This is a fun way to practice control over your pen.

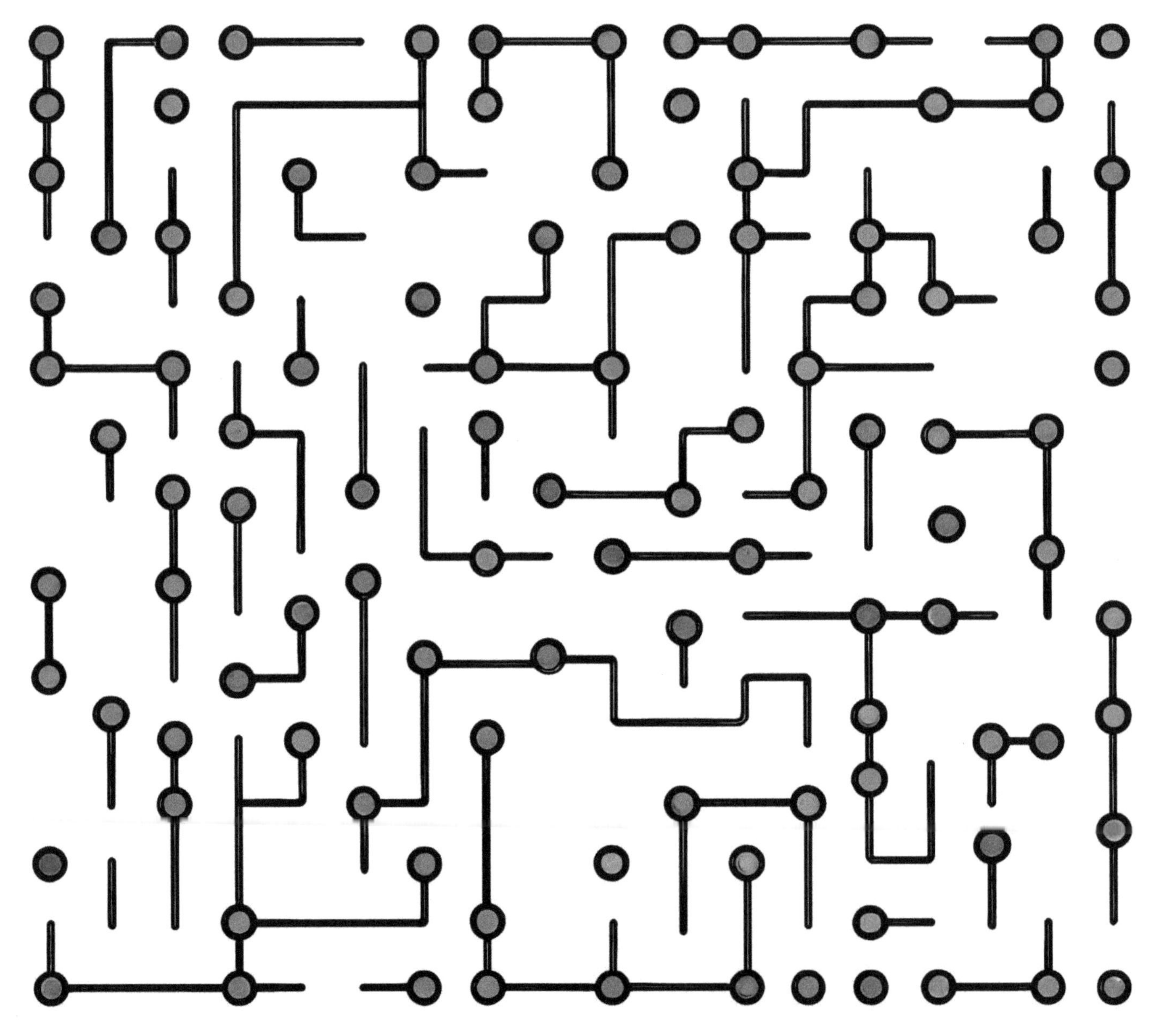

Ready, set, draw!

Making Patterns:

Once you're comfortable, try making patterns with your lines and shapes. Zigzags, waves, loops – let your imagination run wild!

Remember, practice makes perfect! The more you practice these basic shapes and strokes, the better you'll get at calligraphy. And the most important thing? Have fun with it! Each line and curve is a step on your amazing calligraphy adventure.

Ready, set, draw!

Your First Letters

Fantastic job on those shapes and strokes!

Now, let's use them to start forming some letters. This is where we see the magic of calligraphy really come to life. We're going to learn how to write the letters of the alphabet in a simple calligraphy style. Ready to be a letter wizard? Here we go!

Starting with A, B, C: Begin with the first three letters: A, B, and C. Use your curvy and straight lines to form these letters. Remember, 'A' has a sharp peak like a mountain, 'B' has lovely round bellies, and 'C' is like a moon that's not quite full.

Moving Through the Alphabet: After A, B, and C, keep going with the rest of the alphabet. Each letter has its own unique shape and personality. D is like a half-open door, E has three equal horizontal lines, and F is like E but without the bottom line!

Taking Your Time: Some letters will be easier than others, and that's okay! Take your time with each one. If a letter seems tricky, practice it a few more times. You'll get it!

Practice Makes Perfect: The more you practice, the more your letters will start to have that special calligraphy style. They'll look elegant and flowy, just like in storybooks!

Adding a Personal Touch: Once you feel comfortable with each letter, start to add your own little twists and turns to them. Maybe you add a little curl to the end of your 'G' or a swoosh to your 'T'. This is your art, so make it your own!

Write Your Name: A fun exercise is to write your name in calligraphy. See how beautiful it can look when you use the skills you've learned!

Remember, there's no rush. Enjoy the process of learning each letter. Calligraphy is like a dance of the pen on paper – it's all about the flow and the fun. Keep practicing, and soon you'll be able to write the whole alphabet in your own unique, calligraphic style!

Can't wait to see your fabulous letters! Keep up the great work!

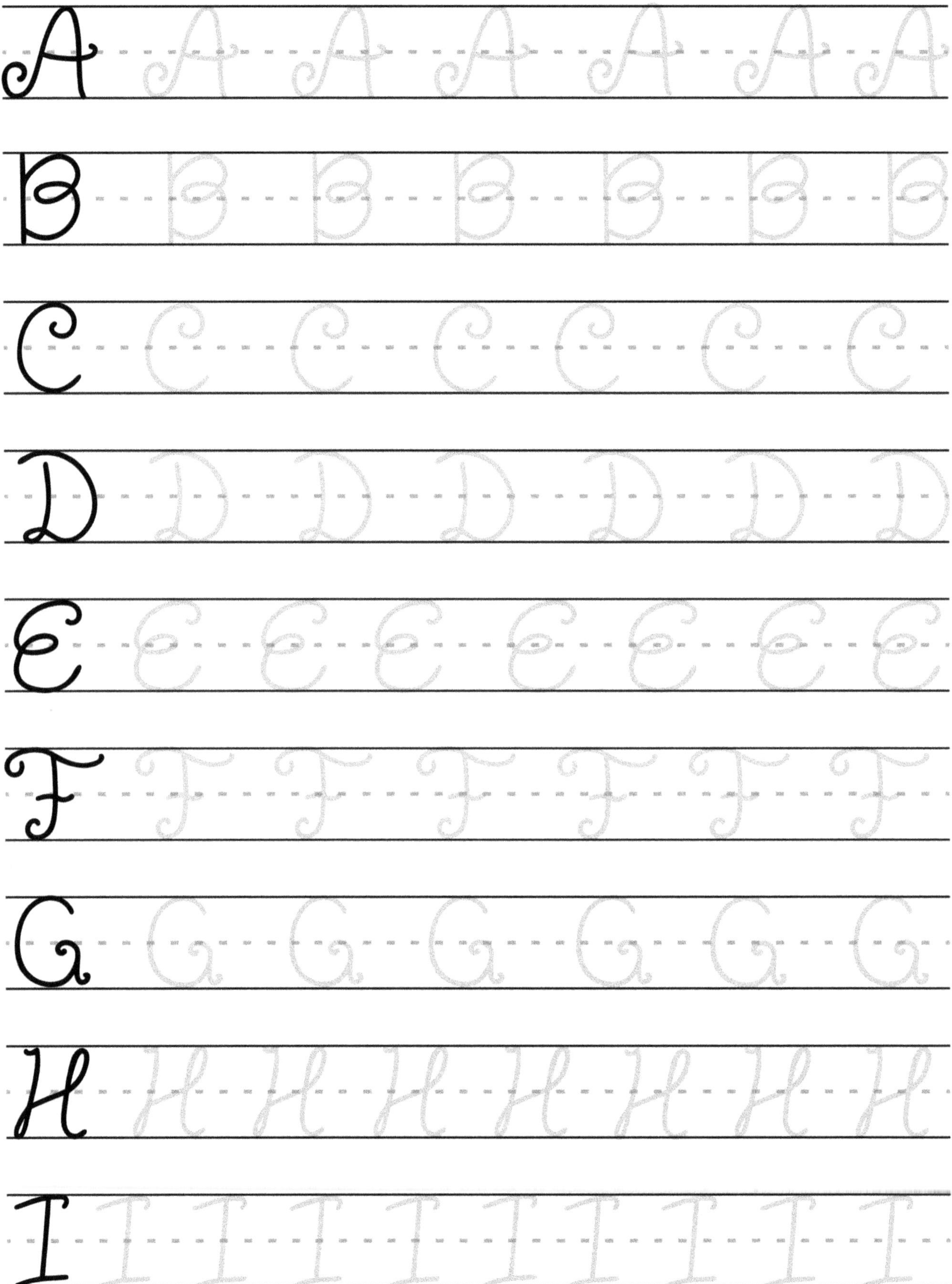
A
B
C
D
E
F
G
H
I

To work now your letters!

A

B

C

D

E

F

G

H

I

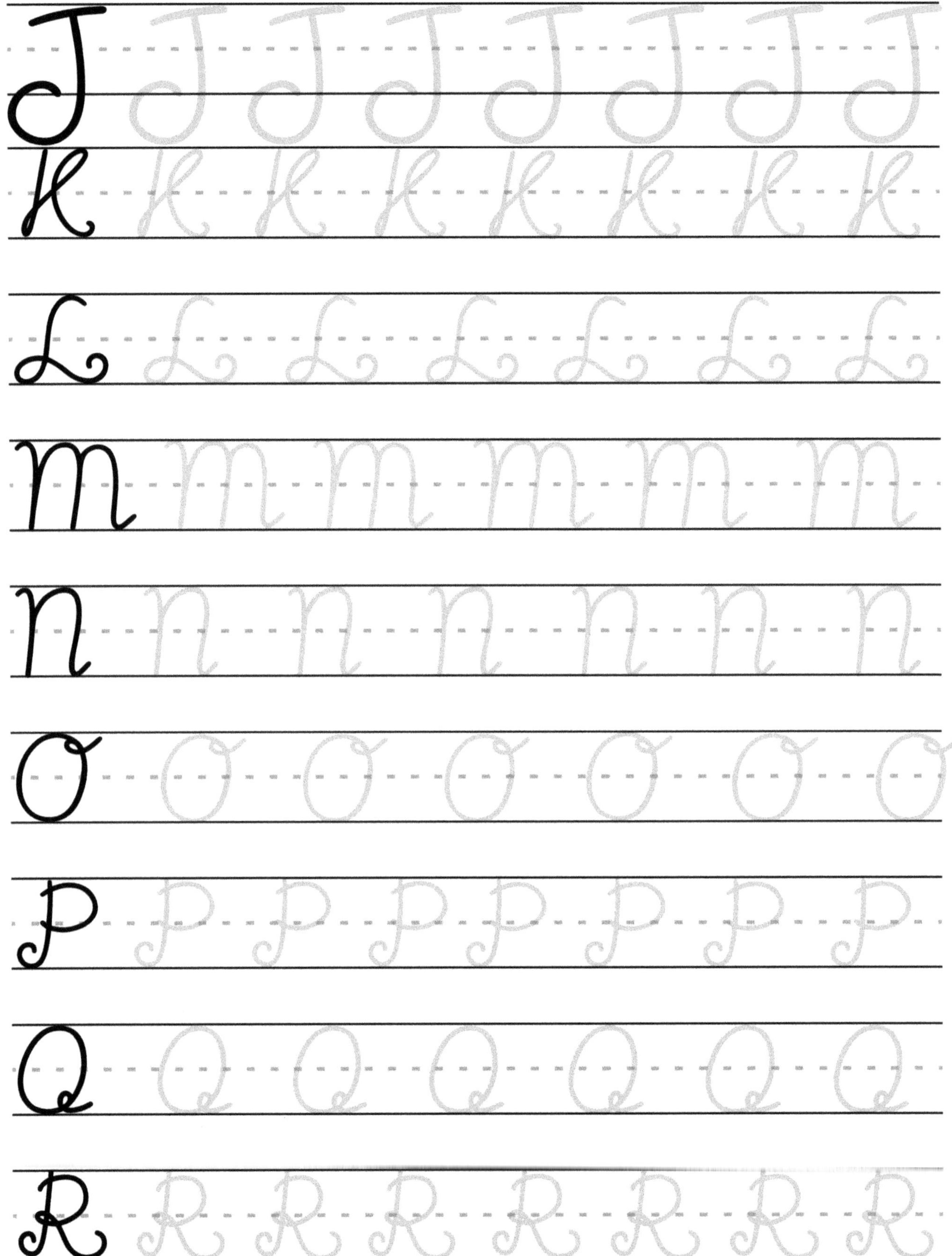

To work now your letters!

J

K

L

M

N

O

P

Q

R

To work now your letters!

S

T

U

V

W

X

Y

Z

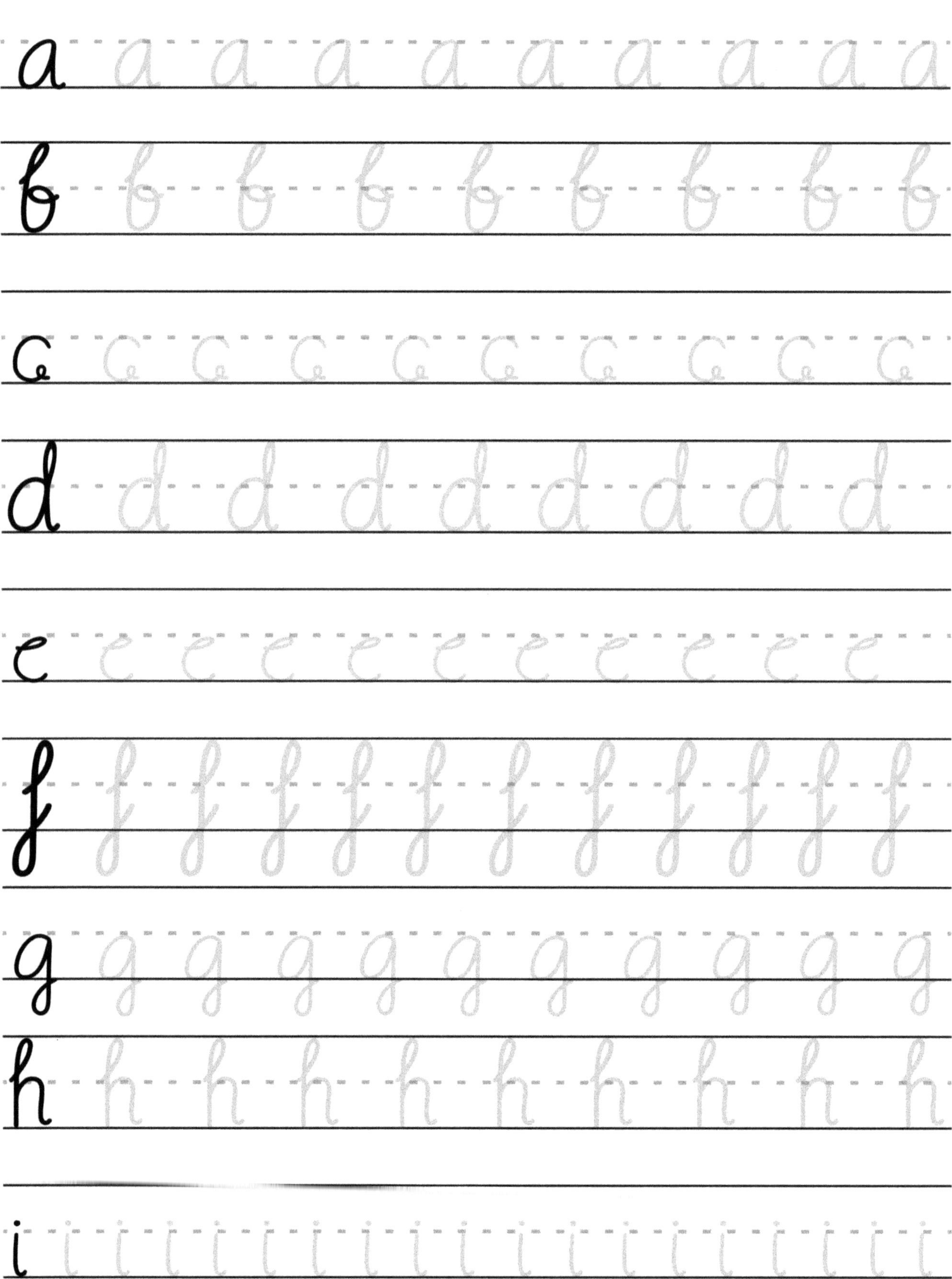

To work now your letters!

a

b

c

d

e

f

g

h

i

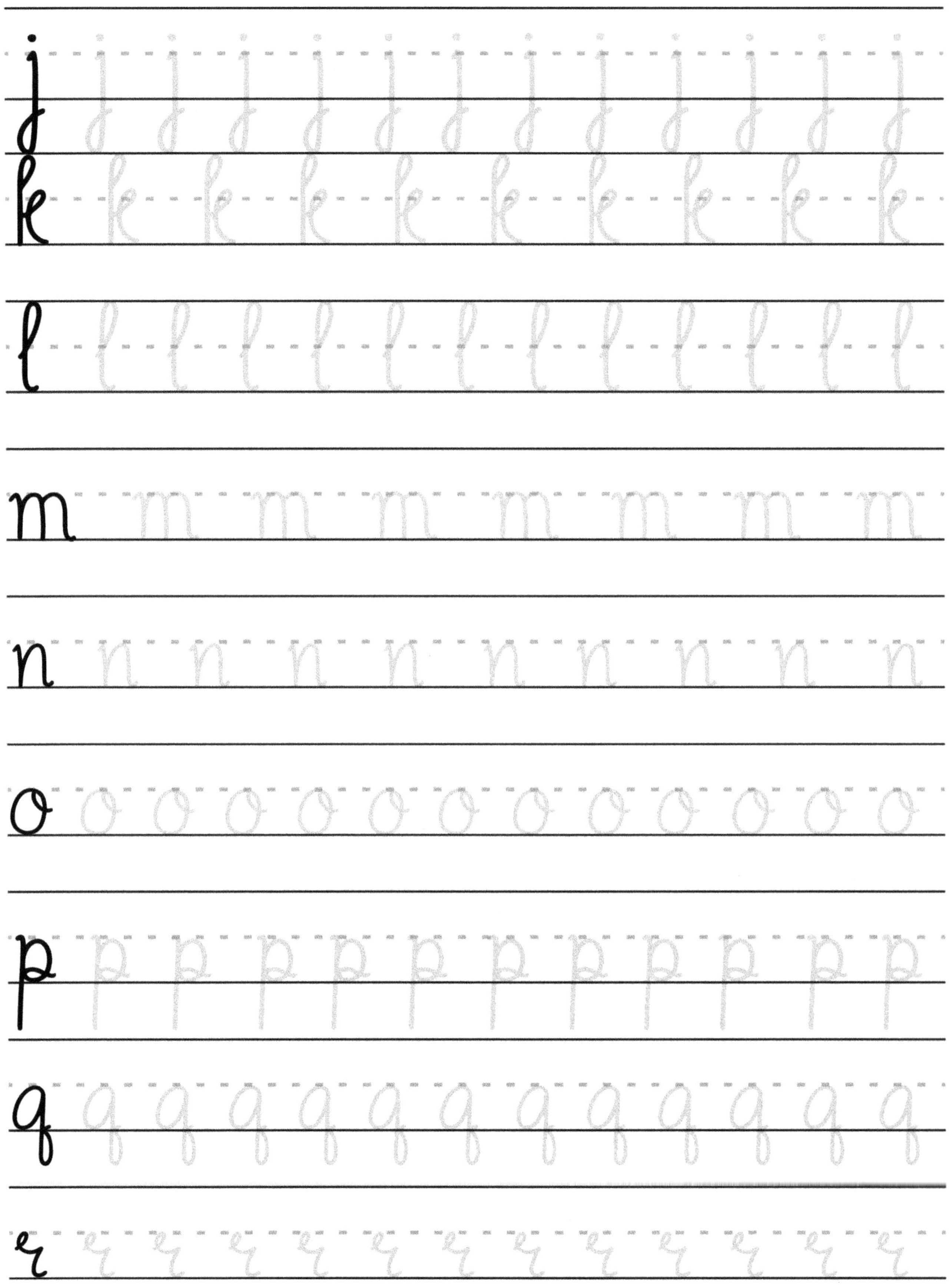

To work now your letters!

j

k

l

m

n

o

p

q

r

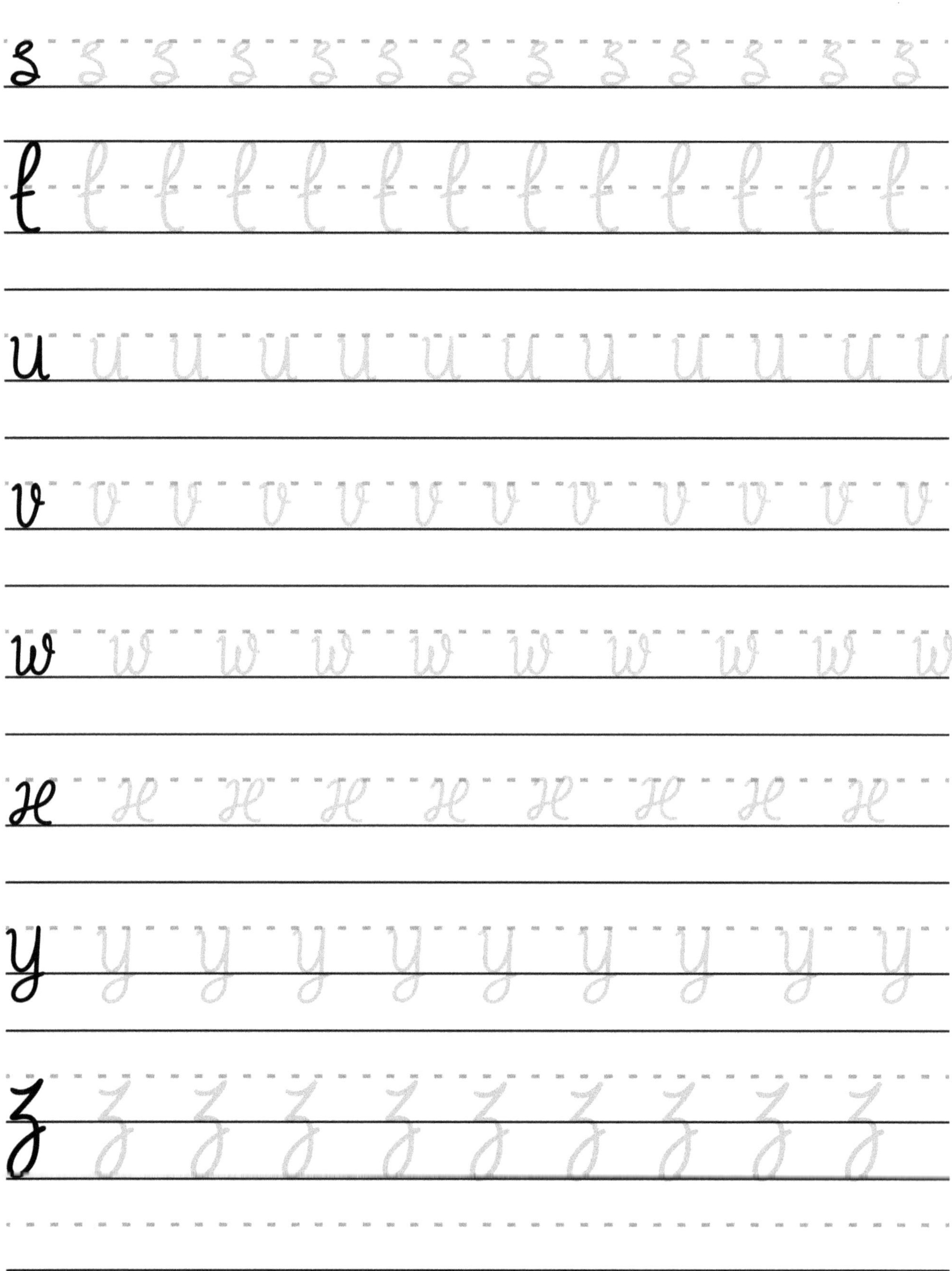

To work now your letters!

s

t

u

v

w

x

y

z

Fun with Words

Great job on learning the letters!

Now, let's put those letters together and have some fun with words. We can create names, simple words, or even short phrases in your new calligraphy style. It's like putting together pieces of a puzzle, but this puzzle is made of beautiful letters! Let's start:

Writing Your Name:

One of the best words to start with is your own name. Write out each letter of your name in calligraphy. Watch how it transforms into something special and unique, just like you!

Emma Emma Emma
Mia Mia Mia Mia
And now your name
Liam Liam Liam
Noah Noah Noah

Olivia Olivia Olivia

Harper Harper

And now your name

Luke Luke Luke

Finn Finn Finn Finn

Sophia Sophia Sophia

Ava Ava Ava Ava

And now your name

Sam Sam Sam Sam

Max Max Max

Your Favorite Words:

Think of words that make you happy. It could be "Sunshine", "Stars", "Play", "Love", "Rainbow", "Friend", "Magic", "Giggle" or "Hug".Write these words in your calligraphy style. Notice how the words look more joyful and lively?

Sunshine Sunshine

Sunshine Sunshine

Sunshine Sunshine

Stars Stars Stars

Stars Stars Stars

Stars Stars Stars

Play Play Play Play

Play Play Play Play

Play Play Play Play

Love Love Love

Love Love Love

Love Love Love

Rainbow Rainbow

Rainbow Rainbow

Rainbow Rainbow

Friend Friend

Friend Friend

Friend Friend

Magic Magic

Magic Magic

Magic Magic

Giggle Giggle

Giggle Giggle

Giggle Giggle

Hug Hug Hug Hug

Hug Hug Hug Hug

Hug Hug Hug Hug

Short Phrases:

Try writing short phrases like "Be Happy", "Dream Big", "Stay Cool", "You Shine", "Stay Strong", "Go Explore", "Be Brave", "Keep Going" or "Shine Bright". Each word combines different letters, giving you good practice and a chance to see how they flow together in a phrase

Be Happy Be Happy

Be Happy Be Happy

Be Happy Be Happy

Dream Big Dream Big

Dream Big Dream Big

Dream Big Dream Big

Stay Cool Stay Cool

Stay Cool Stay Cool

Stay Cool Stay Cool

You Shine You Shine

You Shine You Shine

You Shine You Shine

Stay Strong

Stay Strong

Stay Strong

Go explore Go explore

Go explore Go explore

Go explore Go explore

Be brave Be brave
Be brave Be brave
Be brave Be brave

Keep Going Keep Going
Keep Going Keep Going
Keep Going Keep Going

Shine Bright Shine Bright
Shine Bright Shine Bright
Shine Bright Shine Bright

Greeting Cards:

Use your calligraphy skills to make simple greeting cards. You could write "Happy Birthday", "Thank You", "Best Friends Forever","Congratulations", "Best Wishes", "You're Amazing", "Happy Fun Day", "Super Kid", "So Proud of You", or "Adventure Awaits". Decorate them with drawings or stickers to make them even more special.

Happy Birthday

Happy Birthday

Happy Birthday

Thank You

Thank You

Thank You

Best Friends Forever

Best Friends Forever

Best Friends Forever

Best Friends Forever

Congratulations

Congratulations

Congratulations

Congratulations

Best Wishes

Best Wishes

Best Wishes

Best Wishes

You're Amazing

You're Amazing

You're Amazing

You're Amazing

Happy Fun Day

Happy Fun Day

Happy Fun Day

Super Kid

Super Kid

Super Kid

So Proud of You

So Proud of You

So Proud of You

So Proud of You

Adventure Awaits

Adventure Awaits

Adventure Awaits

Adventure Awaits

THANK
YOU

Thank You!

For all the fun times and
the laughter we share,
For the joy and the
great memories made,
I want to say
a BIG thank you!
You're the best, making
the world brighter.

Word Art:

Turn words into art. Write a word and then decorate it. You can draw stars around "Dream" or flowers around "Joy". Your word is no longer just a word

- it's a work of art!

Dream

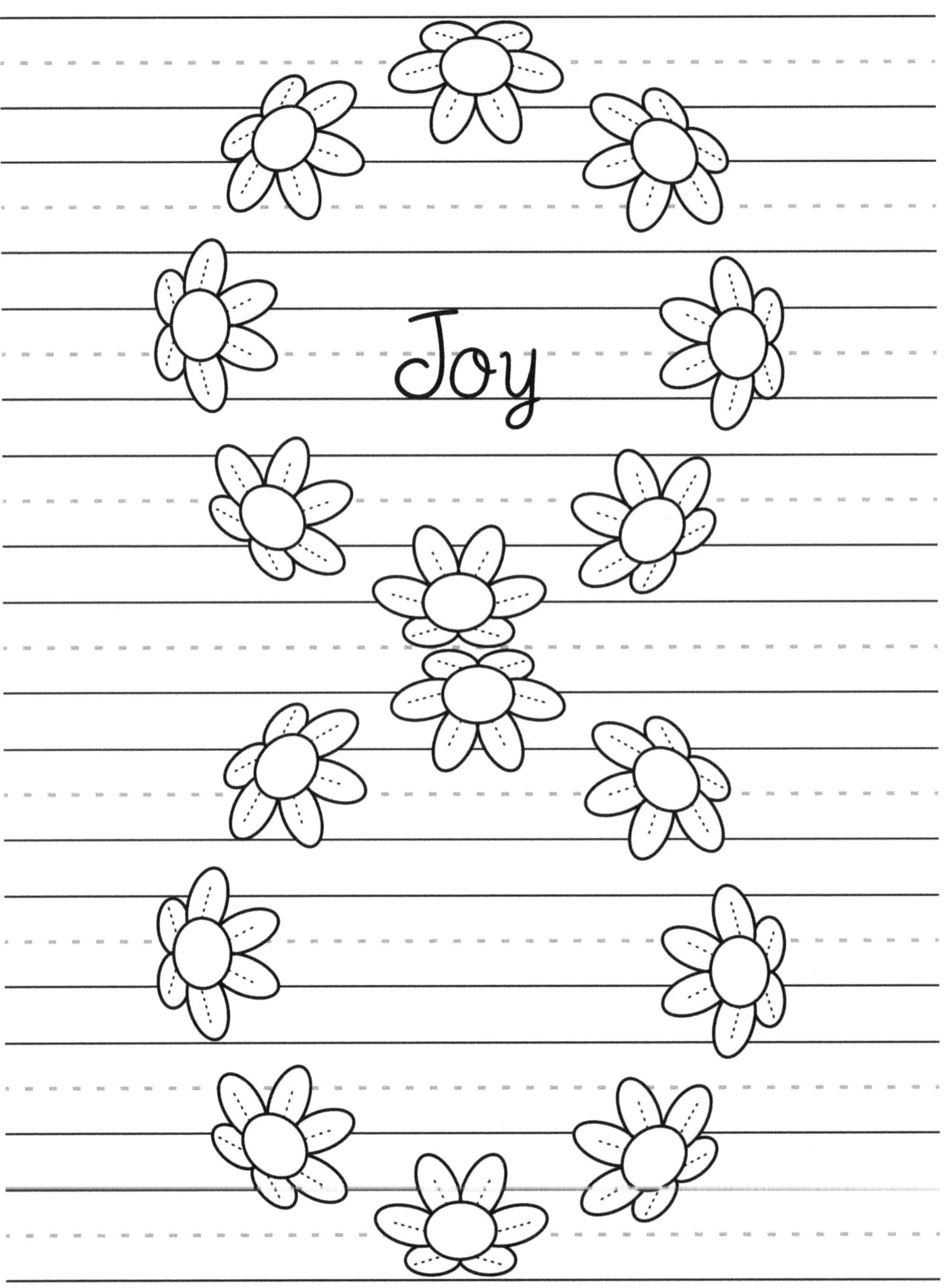
Joy

Love

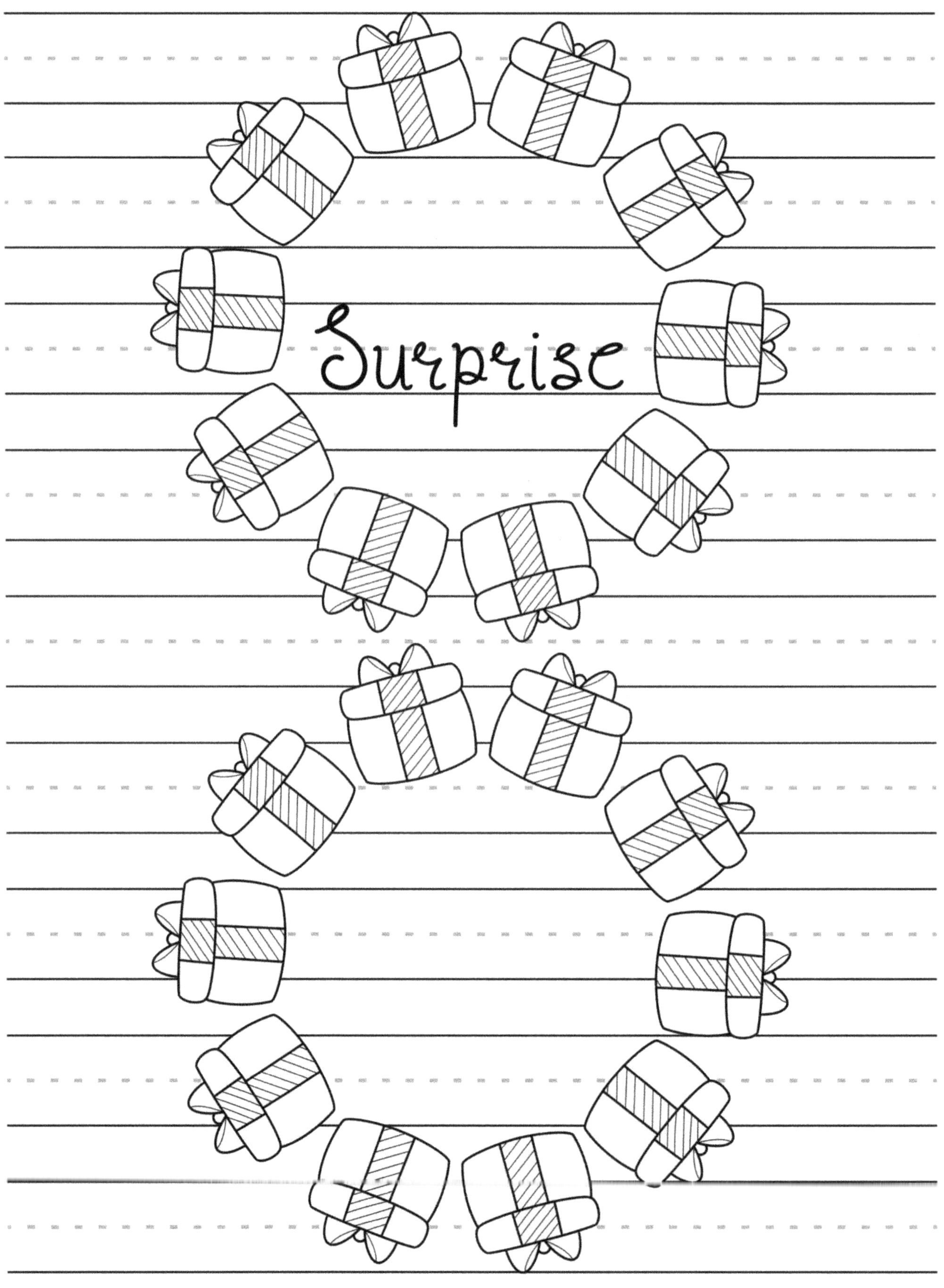
Surprise

Match words to the right decorations: "Help", "Tea"

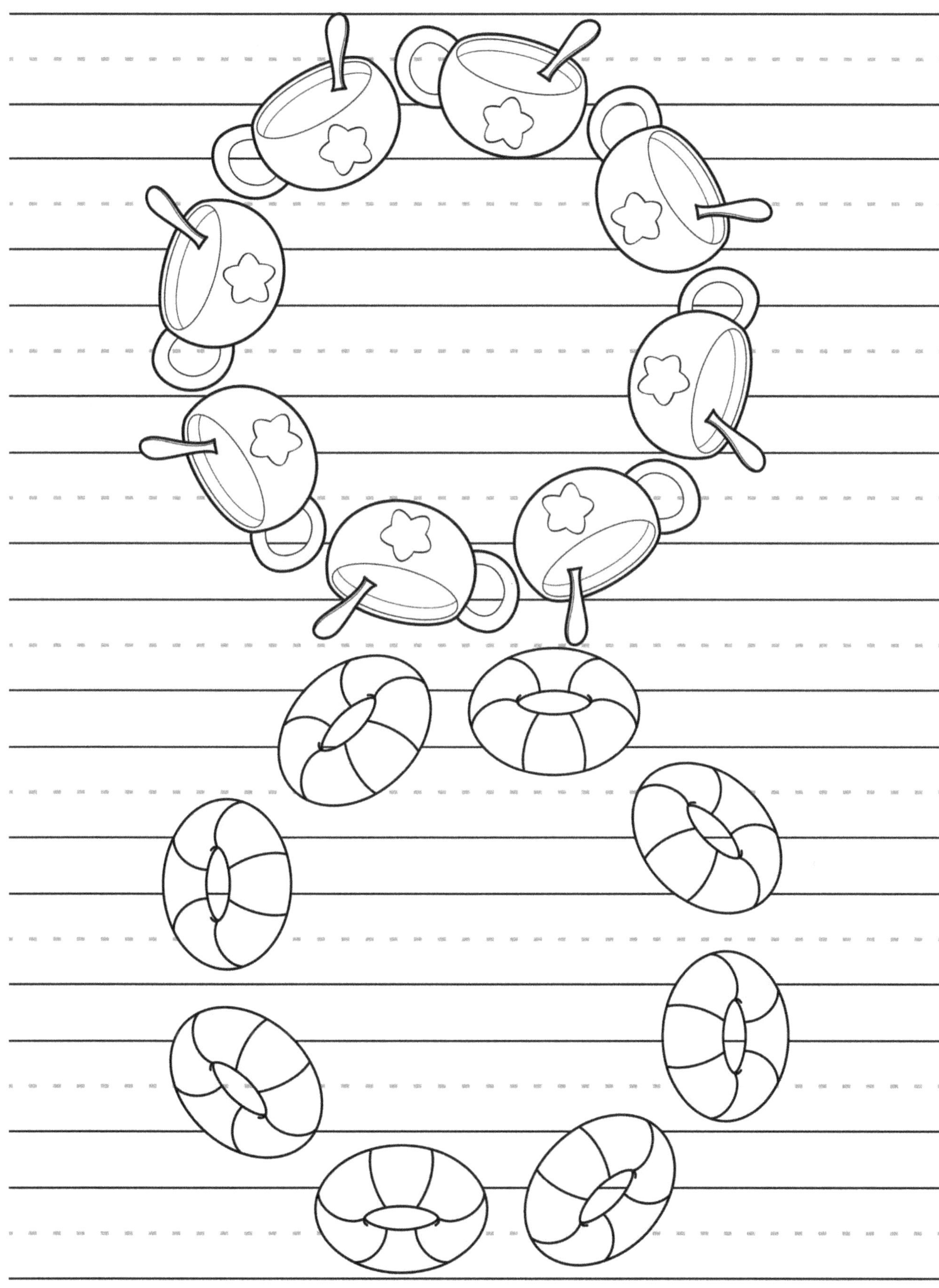

Match words to the right decorations: "Gift", "Sweets"

Match words to the right decorations: "Winter", "Cash"

Fun Challenge:

Calligraphic word splitting:

Choose a long word and split it into shorter words that are hidden in it, representing them in a creative way.

Try writing the word "Heartfelt." In this word you can find several smaller words "Heart", "Hear", "Art", "Ear", "Felt".

"Butterfly", "But", "Butter", "Utter", "Fly".

These fun challenges can be really creative and exciting!

Heartfelt Heartfelt

Heartfelt Heartfelt

Heart Heart Heart

Heart Heart Heart

Hear Hear Hear

Hear Hear Hear

Art Art Art Art

Art Art Art Art

Ear Ear Ear Ear

Car Car Car Car

Felt Felt Felt Felt

Felt Felt Felt Felt

Butterfly Butterfly

Butterfly Butterfly

But But But But

But But But But

Butter Butter Butter

Butter Butter Butter

Utter Utter Utter

Utter Utter Utter

Fly Fly Fly Fly

Fly Fly Fly Fly

Butterfly felt heart.

Butterfly felt heart.

Butterfly felt heart.

Butterfly felt heart.

Remember, the key to calligraphy is to have fun and express yourself. Each word you write is a reflection of your creativity and imagination. There's no right or wrong way to do it – just your way.

So, let's get those pens moving and create some word magic! I can't wait to see the wonderful words you'll come up with! Happy writing!

Let your pen dance with calligraphy fun!

Dream in Color

Dream in Color

Dream in Color

Magic in Words

Magic in Words

Magic in Words

Create Wonder

Create Wonder

Create Wonder

Be Bold, Be Bright
Fly High, Dream Big
Be the Joy

Dare to Dream

Dare to Dream

Dare to Dream

Explore More

Explore More

Explore More

Radiate Positivity

Radiate Positivity

Radiate Positivity

Write your own magic!

Write your own magic!

Write your own magic!

Write your own magic!

Write your own magic!

Write your own magic!

The End of Our Calligraphy Journey (For Now!)

Dear Amazing Young Artist,

Wow, can you believe we've reached the end of our calligraphy adventure together? You've done such an incredible job! I'm so proud of all the beautiful letters, words, and art you've created. You've turned simple strokes into something truly magical.

Thank You for Joining Me

I want to say a big thank you for joining me on this fun journey. It has been a joy to see your skills grow and your creativity shine. Remember, every time you picked up your pen, you were not just writing – you were making art!

Keep Practicing and Exploring

Even though our book is ending, your calligraphy adventure doesn't have to stop here. Keep practicing your letters and words. Keep making cards for your friends and family. And most importantly, keep having fun with your calligraphy!

You Are a Calligraphy Star

You started this book as a beginner, and now look at you – a calligraphy star! I hope you keep your calligraphy pen dancing on the paper, creating more and more beautiful art.

A Final Cheer for You!

Hip, hip, hooray for you and all the wonderful calligraphy you've done! I can't wait to see what you'll create next. Keep being awesome, keep being creative, and keep being you!

Thank you again for spending this time with me. Remember, in the world of calligraphy, every letter is a piece of your heart, and every word tells a story – your story.

Goodbye for Now

So, it's not really goodbye, it's just a 'see you later' as you continue your adventure in calligraphy. Keep that pen moving, and keep your imagination flowing!

P.S.: Don't forget to show off your calligraphy to the world. You're a star!

www.ingramcontent.com/pod-product-compliance
Lightning Source LLC
LaVergne TN
LVHW071452180726
843512LV00018B/1356

* 9 7 8 8 3 9 6 9 9 5 1 2 4 *